ANIMAL TRACKS
of Alaska

ANIMAL TRACKS
of Alaska

by Chris Stall

THE
MOUNTAINEERS

First edition: first printing 1993, second printing 1995, third printing 1997, fourth printing 1999

No part of this book may be reproduced in any form, or by any electronic, mechanical, or other means, without permission in writing from the publisher.

Published by The Mountaineers
1001 SW Klickitat Way, Suite 201, Seattle, Washington 98134

Manufactured in the United States of America

Book design by Watson Graphics
Author photo by Angela Staubach
Track on cover: Brown Bear

Library of Congress Cataloging in Publication Data

Stall, Chris.
    Animal tracks of Alaska / by Chris Stall.
            p.   cm.
    Includes bibliographical references (p.   ) and index.
    1. Animal Tracks–Alaska–Identification.   I. Title.
    QL768.S725   1993
    599'.09798–dc20   92-45130
                                                           CIP

Contents

Preface

Most people don't get a chance to observe animals in the wild, with the exceptions of road kills and a few nearly tame species in parks and campgrounds. Many wild animals are nocturnal or scarce, and many are shy and secretive to avoid the attention of predators, or stealthy as they stalk their next meal. In addition, most wild creatures are extremely wary of humans either instinctively or because they've learned through experience to be that way. We may catch fortuitous glimpses now and then, but few of us have the time or motivation required for lengthy journeys into wild country for the sole purpose of locating animals. The result is that areas where we would expect to see animals often seem practically devoid of wildlife.

That's rarely the case, of course. Actually, many animals reside in or pass through all reasonably wild habitats. Though we may not see them, they nevertheless leave indications of their passage. But for the most part such signs are obscure or confusing so that only the most experienced and knowledgeable wilderness travelers notice them.

There's one grand exception: *animal tracks*. Often readily apparent even to the most casual and inexperienced observer, tracks not only indicate the presence of wild animals but can also be matched relatively easily with the animals that made them. I guess that's why I have been fascinated by animal tracks since my childhood in rural New York, and why that focus has continued through two decades of wandering and searching for them in wild lands all across North America.

Animal Tracks of Alaska is a compilation of eleven years of living in Alaska, and many miles of my own field work, protracted observations, sketching, photography, and research into a mountain of articles and books too numerous to list—and too heavy to carry into the backcountry.

Animal tracks may be something you concern yourself with only when you happen upon them, or your interest in tracks may become nearly obsessive. You may find yourself hiking with your chin resting securely on your chest, feverishly scanning the ground for clues. You may seek out snow because tracks show up on it better than most other surfaces. In the absence of snow, you might find yourself altering your routes, avoiding bedrock and ground cover, and seeking out damp sand, soft dirt, and mud along streams, near ponds and lakes, and around swamps. After a rainfall, you might make special trips to check fresh mud, knowing that among evidence of human activity the animal prints will be clear and precise.

Whatever your degree of interest, I hope you will enjoy using this book, in your backyard or in the wildest and most remote regions of Alaska, and that your interest in identifying tracks grows until you reach the level of knowledge at which you no longer need this book.

Good luck!

Chris Stall
Cincinnati, Ohio

Introduction

HOW TO USE THIS BOOK

1. When you first locate an unknown track, look around the immediate area to locate the clearest imprint (see Tracking Tips below). You can usually find at least one imprint or even a partial print distinct enough for counting toes, noting the shape of the heel pad, determining the presence or absence of claw marks, and so on.

2. Decide what kind of animal is most likely to have made the tracks; then turn to one of the two main sections of this book. The first and largest features mammals; the second, much shorter section is devoted entirely to birds.

3. Measure an individual track, using the ruler printed on the back cover of this book. Tracks of roughly 5 inches or less are illustrated life-size; those larger than 5 inches have been reduced as necessary to fit on the pages.

4. Flip quickly through the appropriate section until you find tracks that are about the same *size* as your mystery tracks. The tracks are arranged roughly by size from smallest to largest.

5. Search carefully for the tracks in the size range that, as closely as possible, match the *shape* of the unknown tracks.

6. If you find the right shape but the size depicted in the book is too big, remember that the illustrations represent tracks of an average *adult* animal.

Perhaps your specimen was made by a young animal. Search some more: on the ground nearby you might locate the tracks of a parent, which will more closely match the size of the illustration.

7. Read the comments on range, habitat, and behavior, to help confirm the identification.

This book is intended to assist you in making field identifications of commonly encountered animal tracks. To keep the book compact, my remarks are limited to each animal's most obvious characteristics. By all means enhance your own knowledge of these track makers. Libraries and book stores are good places to begin learning more about wild animals. Visits to zoos with Alaskan wildlife on display can also be worthwhile educational experiences. And there's no substitute for firsthand field study. You've found tracks; now you know what animals to look for. Read my notes on diet, put some bait out, sit quietly downwind with binoculars for a few hours, and see what comes along. Or follow the tracks a while. Use your imagination and common sense, and you'll be amazed at how much you can learn, and how rewarding the experiences can be.

As you use this book, remember that track identification is an inexact science. The illustrations in this book represent average *adult* tracks on *ideal* surfaces. But many of the tracks you encounter in the wild will be those of smaller-than-average animals, particularly in late spring and early summer. There are also larger-than-average animals, and injured or deformed ones, and animals that act unpredictably. Some creatures walk sideways on occasion. Most vary their gait so that in a single set of tracks front prints may fall ahead, behind, or beneath the rear. In addition, ground conditions are usually less than ideal in the wild, and animals often dislodge debris, which may further confuse the picture. Use this book as a guide, and anticipate lots of variations.

In attempting to identify tracks, remember that their size can vary greatly depending on the type of ground surface—sand that is loose or firm, wet or dry; a thin layer of mud over hard earth; deep soft mud; various lightly frozen surfaces; firm or loose dirt; dry or moist snow; a dusting of snow or frost over various surfaces; and so on. Note the surface from which the illustrations are taken and interpret what you should find in nature accordingly.

You should also be aware that droplets from trees, windblown debris, and the like often leave a variety of marks on the ground that could be mistaken for animal tracks. While studying tracks, look around for and be aware of nonanimal factors that might have left "tracks" of their own.

The range notes pertain only to Alaska. Many trackmakers in this book also live elsewhere in North America. Range and habitat remarks are general guidelines because both are subject to change, from variations in both animal and human populations, climatic factors, pollution levels, acts of God, and so forth.

The size, height, and weight listed for each animal are those for average adults. Size refers to length from nose to tip of tail; height, the distance from ground to shoulder.

A few well-known species have been left out of this book: bats and many sea mammals, for example, which leave no tracks. Some species herein, particularly small rodents and birds, stand as representatives of groups of related species. In such cases the featured species is the one most commonly encountered and widely distributed. Related species, often with similar tracks, are listed in the notes. Where their tracks can be distinguished, guidelines for doing so are provided.

If you encounter an injured animal or an apparently orphaned infant, you may be tempted to take it home and care for it. Do not do so. Instead, report the animal to local authorities, who are better able to care for it. In addition, federal and state laws often strictly control the handling of wild animals. This is always the case with species classified as *rare* or *endangered*. Animals are better left in the wild, and to do otherwise may be illegal.

TRACKING TIPS

At times you'll be lucky enough to find a perfectly clear and precise track that gives you all the information you need to identify the maker with a quick glance through this book. More often the track will be imperfect or fragmented. Following the tracks may lead you to a more readily identifiable print. Or maybe you have the time and inclination to follow an animal whose identity you already know in order to learn more about its habits, characteristics, and behavior.

Here are some tips for improving your tracking skills:

1. If you don't see tracks, look for disturbances—leaves or twigs in

unnatural positions, debris or stones that appear to have been moved or turned. Stones become bleached on top over time, so a stone with its darker side up or sideways has recently been dislodged.

2. Push small sticks into the ground to mark individual signs. These will help you keep your bearings and "map out" the animal's general direction of travel.

3. Check immovable objects such as trees, logs, and boulders along the route of travel for scratches, scuff marks, or fragments of hair.

4. Look at the ground from different angles, from standing height, from kneeling height, and, if possible, from an elevated position in a tree or on a boulder or rise.

5. On very firm surfaces, place your cheek on the ground and observe the surface, first through one eye, then the other, looking for unnatural depressions or disturbances.

6. Study the trail from as many different directions as possible. Trail signs may become obvious as the angle of light between them and your eyes changes, especially if dew, dust, or rain covers some parts of the ground surface.

7. Check for tracks beneath recently disturbed leaves or fallen debris.

8. Try not to focus your attention so narrowly that you lose sight of the larger patterns of the country around you.

9. Keep your bearings. Some animals circle back if they become aware of being followed. If you find yourself following signs in a circular path, try waiting motionless and silent for a while, observing behind you.

10. Look ahead as far as possible as you follow signs. Animals take the paths of least resistance, so look for trails or runways. You may even catch sight of your quarry.

11. Animals are habitual in their movements among burrows, den sites, sources of water and wood, temporary shelters, prominent trees, and so on. As you track and look ahead, try to anticipate where the creature might be going.

12. Stalk as you track; move as carefully and quietly as possible.

The secrets to successful tracking are patience and knowledge. Whenever you see an animal leaving tracks, go look at them and note the activity you observed. When you find and identify tracks, make little sketches alongside the book's illustrations, showing cluster patterns, or individual impressions that are different from those drawn. Make notes about what you learn in the wilds and from other readings. Eventually, you will build a body of knowledge from your own experience, and your future attempts at track identification will become easier and more certain.

This book is largely a compilation of my personal experiences. Your experiences with certain animals and their tracks may be identical, similar, or quite different. If you notice a discrepancy or find tracks that are not included in this book, carefully note your observations, or even amend the illustrations or text to reflect your own experiences. This book is intended for use in the field as a tool for identifying animal tracks of Alaska.

Mammals
Amphibians
Invertebrates

INVERTEBRATES

The smallest track impressions you are likely to encounter in nature will probably look something like those illustrated at the right.

From left to right, the illustration shows tracks of two common beetles, a centipede, and a cricket. The track of an earthworm crosses from lower left to the upper right corner.

You might initially mistake a variety of scuffs and scratches left by windblown or otherwise dislodged debris, the imprint of raindrops that have fallen from overhanging limbs, impressions left by the smallest mice, or even the perplexing calligraphy of toads for insect marks. If you have more than a square foot or so of ground surface to scrutinize, however, you will usually find that the insect tracks form a recognizably connected line; the extremely shallow depth of the trail of imprints is also a good clue that a very lightweight being has passed by.

With literally millions of species out there, trying to identify the insect that made a particular track can be challenging, but there are times when you can follow a trail and find, at the end, either the bug itself, or a burrow that could yield its resident with a little patient and careful excavation on your part. If you spend enough time in one area, you will begin to observe specific species in the act of making their tracks, and that goes a long way toward track recognition—for any size of animal.

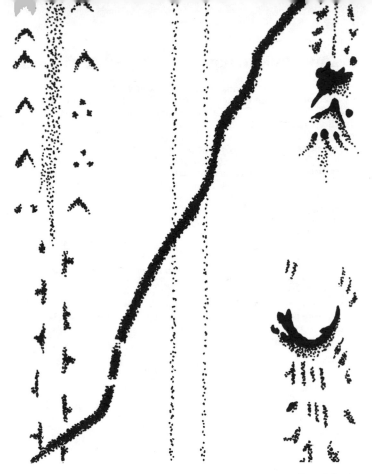

Invertebrates
life size in mud

MEADOW JUMPING MOUSE   *Zapus hudsonius*

Order: Rodentia (gnawing mammals). **Family:** Zapodidae (jumping mice). **Range and habitat:** southeastern and southern Alaska; in moist fields and lush grassy areas, also thickets and woods at medium to higher elevations and mountain fringes. **Size and weight:** 9 inches; 1 ounce. **Diet:** insects, grasses, seeds, berries, and fungi. **Sounds:** frequent chirps at night among members of foraging groups.

The meadow jumping mouse varies in color from yellowish to reddish, with a very long, white-tipped tail and relatively large, strong hind legs and feet. It is not easy to sight in the wild because it is generally nocturnal during warm weather and hibernates for 6 to 8 months during long, cold winters. Occasionally, as you hike off-trail, you might startle one and see it bound away in 3- to 4-foot leaps before disappearing again into the ground cover.

The tracks of this jumping mouse are quite distinctive and should be easy to identify, even if the imprints are not very clear, because it is the only mouse living in the habitat described above that takes single jumps, or several in a series, of 3 to 5 feet each. Rear-foot impressions will be noticeably longer (around $1/2$ inch) than those of other similar-sized creatures, and its long tail leaves marks more frequently (either among the footprints or out to the side). But when leaping in a series of bounds, only the hind feet contact the ground, leaving a trail of small, widely spaced print-pairs without tail drag marks, also unique.

Meadow Jumping Mouse
life size in mud

17

MASKED SHREW   *Sorex cinereus*

Order: Insectivora (insect-eating mammals, including shrews, moles, and bats). **Family:** Soricidae (shrews). **Range and habitat:** throughout Alaska; in moist areas in forests and meadows. **Size and weight:** 5 inches; 1 ounce. **Diet:** insects, small animals, and carrion. **Sounds:** generally silent; occasional diminutive squeaks.

The masked shrew, the most wide-ranging Alaskan shrew, lives a life of gluttony. Due to the high rate of shrew metabolism, it must eat an amount of food equivalent to its own body weight every twenty-four hours. It eats around the clock summer and winter alike, usually every two to three hours.

Other Alaskan shrews include the water shrew, found in and around fresh water of southeastern and south central Alaska; the arctic shrew, a docile tricolored shrew living in swamps and meadows of west, central, and northern Alaska; and the pygmy shrew (the smallest mammal in North America!), found in the deep forests of the central and southern parts of the state. All are very similar in proportion to the masked shrew, and field sightings will help you identify locally prevalent species.

Primarily because shrews are so light in weight, it is unusual to find shrew tracks unless the animals have been scurrying over fresh, fine mud or snow. Their tiny tracks are seen everywhere after a snowfall. Shrew tracks might be confused with those of various mice, but close inspection will reveal shrew trails to be at least $1/2$ inch narrower than most mice trails. Also, shrew tracks generally have an etched unbroken line between the pairs of miniscule footprints, caused by the dragging tail.

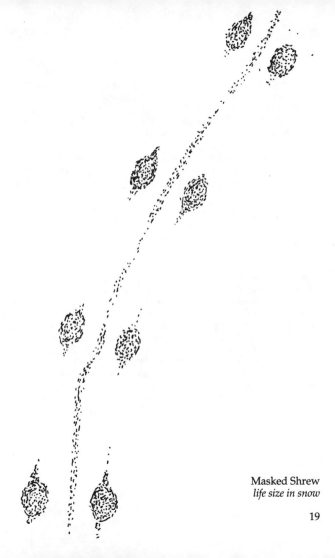

Masked Shrew
life size in snow

19

TUNDRA VOLE

Microtus oeconomus

Order: Rodentia (gnawing mammals). **Family:** Cricetidae (New World rats and mice). **Range and habitat:** throughout Alaska; in tundra areas around fresh water, marshes, and drier grassy places. **Size and weight:** 6 inches; 4 ounces. **Diet:** grain, grasses, bulbs, bark, flowers, and seeds. **Sounds:** generally quiet; occasional small squeaks.

On a camping trip, you might awake one morning to see a tundra vole stealthily making trips back and forth from your food cache. Closer inspection at the scene of the "crime" will show that the vole has gnawed a hole in your bag of granola. Bit by bit it is spiriting away the contents of the bag.

Voles are plump, sprightly little balls of dark gray or brown fur. They go about their activities year-round, eating by day and night. And do not be surprised if you see voles moving around in water. They are expert swimmers and use their aquatic skills to cross streams and travel in marshy areas.

Several other species of voles and volelike animals live in portions of Alaska, including the widespread meadow vole of central, south, and southeastern Alaska; the yellow-cheeked vole of east central Alaska; and the singing vole, or "Alaskan vole," which trills from burrows around most of the state above timberline; as well as three species of lemmings. All are nearly indistinguishable from the tundra vole in appearance, habits, and tracks. Careful field observations are required to determine the exact identity of specific track makers in each particular locale.

Vole tracks in mud show the four toes on the front paw and the five toes on the back. The distance between track clusters changes with speed, but generally averages 2 to 3 inches. Voles are inclined to a ground-hugging mode of travel. Mice, on the other hand, generally travel in leaps, averaging 5 to 6 inches between track groups.

Tundra Vole
life size in dust

BOREAL TOAD
Western toad

Bufo boreas

Order: Salientia (frogs, toads, and allies). **Family:** Bufonidae (true toads). **Range and habitat:** throughout southeastern Alaska; in all moist coastal forests and adjoining areas, wherever insects are abundant, usually but not necessarily within a mile of permanent dampness. **Size and weight:** 4 inches; 2 ounces. **Diet:** insects. **Sounds:** high-pitched musical trills.

Toads are small, froglike animals with dry, warty skin, in a variety of reddish, brown, and gray colors. They are primarily nocturnal, but can be seen at dawn or dusk, or even by day. The boreal toad is the only toad in North America living as far north as Alaska.

Unlike frogs, toads often travel fairly far from sources of water. They do require water for breeding, however; look for their long, ropy strings of eggs in stagnant pond water.

Individual toad tracks can be confusing and might be mistaken for the tiny dimples and scratchings of tracks left by small mice or insects. A toad tends to sit quietly waiting for insects to fly past it, at which time it takes a few leaps in the direction of the wing noise, snares the bug with its long, sticky tongue, then repeats the procedure. Thus it may change direction of travel abruptly and often, commonly backtracking over earlier prints, which can make a very confusing picture on the ground.

Toad tracks generally consist of nothing more distinct than a trail of little holes and scrapes, with impressions that sometimes resemble little toad hands. The distinguishing characteristics are the mode of wandering, the short rows of four or five round dimples left by the toes of the larger rear feet, and the drag marks often left by the feet as the toad moves forward; those toe-drag marks point in the direction of travel.

You won't get warts from handling toads, but make sure you don't have insect repellent or other caustic substances on your hands that might injure the toad's sensitive skin.

Boreal Toads
life size in mud

23

WOOD FROG   *Rana sylvatica*

Order: Salientia (frogs, toads, and allies). **Family:** Ranidae (true frogs).
Range and habitat: southeastern, southern, and central Alaska; in moist woods, open grassy areas, and tundra. **Size and weight:** 3 inches; 2 ounces.
Diet: insects. **Sounds:** series of short-duration, raspy, bleated noises.

The wood frog is a small pink, tan, or brown frog with an easily visible dark mask across its face, and a white belly with dark spots. It is the only frog living north of the Arctic Circle in North America. It often travels far from water during the summer months, and hibernates during winter.

The Latin name *Rana* for the genus of this frog is derived from a Sanskrit root, meaning "one who utters a sound." The wood frog uses its voice above and below water. This active, glistening amphibian eats enormous amounts of insects during its lifetime, which makes it especially precious to those who hike in the woodlands. As with the boreal toad, be sure your hands are free of insect repellent when handling this animal.

Wood frogs have long muscular legs and excel in jumping, as their tracks show. The tracks might be confused with the toad's, but toads usually walk rather than hop.

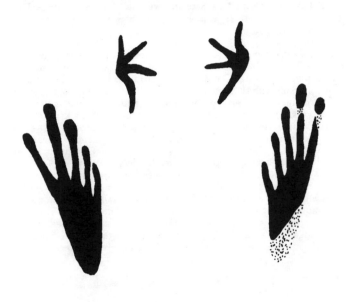

Wood Frog
life size in mud

COLLARED PIKA
Cony

Ochotona collaris

Order: Lagomorpha (rabbitlike mammals). **Family:** Ochotonidae (pikas). **Range and habitat:** mountainous portions of southeastern Alaska; in scree slopes and rock slides. **Size and weight:** 8 inches; 6 ounces. **Diet:** grasses and herbaceous vegetation. **Sounds:** series of short squeaks, warning of danger.

In scree slopes along the roads, you may see ground squirrels and pikas together, but more than likely you'll have to climb a talus slope to find these guinea piglike creatures. But then there's no mistaking pikas, little grayish brown furballs with short round ears and no tail showing, usually sitting quietly in the sun on a promontory or moving quite fluidly over the rocky shards. Pikas spend their summers making little haystacks of clipped vegetation that dry in the sun among the rocks. The hay serves as food supplies for the winter, when the pika remains active but often stays below the snow surface. Its peculiar call is also distinctive and might puzzle you when you hear it coming up from beneath a deep snow cover.

Pika tracks are not easy to locate because this small relative of rabbits and hares lives primarily among rocks and—in winter—beneath snow surfaces, but occasionally you will find them on early-fall or late-spring snow, or in mud around alpine ponds near the animal's stony home. The pika's hairy feet and toes—five front and four rear—and shuffling gait produce what looks like miniature bear tracks; its running trails are composed of clusters not more than 3 inches wide and usually about 10 inches apart.

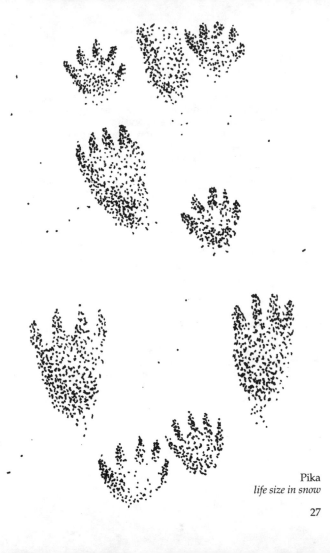

Pika
life size in snow

SHORT-TAILED WEASEL
LEAST WEASEL

Mustela erminea
Mustela nivalis

Order: Carnivora (flesh-eating mammals). **Family:** Mustelidae (weasels and skunks). **Range and habitat:** widespread throughout Alaska; in varied grasslands, wetlands, farmlands, and brushy or wooded terrain to above timberline; usually near water. **Size and weight:** 12 inches; 6 ounces. **Diet:** rodents, including ground squirrels, red squirrels, shrews, voles, lemmings, birds, and baby hares. **Sounds:** generally silent; occasionally squeals.

The short-tailed weasel is an inquisitive and aggressive little carnivore with a thin, elongated body and short, bushy tail. Brown with a white underside and feet during the summer months, in winter the weasel turns almost entirely white, save for the tip of its tail, which remains black. In this fur the short-tailed weasel is commonly known as an ermine.

Short-tailed weasels, like all mustelids, have five toes on each foot, but the imprint of the fifth may be absent. They bound around on the ground most of the time, but also walk along fallen logs, climb trees, and chase prey into water. Usually the rear feet fall over the imprints of the front feet, leaving a line of double tracks distinctive of the smaller weasels. Sometimes, weasels may also leave a variety of track clusters as they dart about searching for food.

The least weasel, a slightly smaller version of the ermine, occupies the same range. The least weasel is the smallest carnivore in North America, feeding mostly on voles and lemmings. The tracks of the two species can be differentiated as follows: ermine track clusters are about 3 inches wide and not much more than 13 inches apart when running; least weasel track clusters are about 1$^1/_2$ inches wide by 3 inches long, with up to 10 inches between clusters.

Short-tailed Weasel
life size in mud

RED SQUIRREL
Pine Squirrel

Tamiasciurus hudsonicus

Order: Rodentia (gnawing mammals). **Family:** Sciuridae (squirrels). **Range and habitat:** throughout most of Alaska; in coniferous forests. **Size and weight:** 12 inches; 9 ounces. **Diet:** pine and spruce cone seeds, willow catkin seeds, fruits, nuts, fungi, insects, buds, and flowers. **Sounds:** scolds, chatters, and churrs.

The red squirrel has a reddish gray coat above and white underneath, and is the only tree squirrel living in Alaska that is active during the day; the northern flying squirrel is nocturnal. These squirrels are active all day and at all times of the year. They are especially busy during the early fall. On a September walk through the woods, you might hear mysterious thumping sounds. Look to the top of an eighty-foot spruce tree where a red squirrel may be energetically heaving cones to the ground like a gnome-sized dock-worker unloading freight. It will pitch cones for a while, then scamper down the trunk to gather them for its winter food cache.

Red squirrel tracks have definite toenail imprints, because squirrels have curved toenails that act as hooks for tree climbing. The track shows the squirrel's four toes on its front foot and five toes on its hind foot. Oftentimes the heel mark will not show. Spacing between the tracks may vary widely, as squirrels leap from 8 to 30 inches.

Red Squirrel
life size in mud

ARCTIC GROUND SQUIRREL
Parka squirrel

Spermophilus parryii

Order: Rodentia (gnawing mammals). **Family:** Sciuridae (squirrels). **Range and habitat:** throughout most of Alaska except permafrost areas; in most open brushy areas and meadows, dry and sandy soils in or adjoining areas of green vegetation (including farmland). **Size and weight:** 15 inches; $3/4$ to $1^1/2$ pounds. **Diet:** omnivorous, including green vegetation, some grains, seeds, fruits, birds, bird eggs, insects, and carrion, as well as its own species. **Sounds:** brief and abrupt high-pitched chirps and whistles.

The arctic ground squirrel is the largest North American ground squirrel and the only one living in Alaska. It is a colonial animal, denning in burrows or occasionally beneath rocks, logs, and stumps, where it stores food. They have several den entrances, each about 3 inches in diameter. arctic ground squirrels are generally gray or buff to reddish, with various subtle coat patterns.

The truncated inner toe on the front foot often leaves a slight imprint on soft surfaces. Eight to 16 inches separate groups of four prints made by running animals; they usually walk only at den entrances where you may find the spacing between individual prints totally random. Ground squirrels seem to be more flat-footed than tree squirrels, and ground squirrel tracks never go far from, and always lead back to, their burrows. Also, ground squirrel claws are fairly straight and usually don't leave marks, whereas tree squirrels have curved claws, adapted to vertical climbing and clinging to bark, which tend to leave tiny marks. Finally, tree squirrels are active all winter; while ground squirrel tracks may be encountered in early fall or late spring snow, they will be absent for the winter.

Arctic Ground Squirrel
life size in mud

NORTHERN FLYING SQUIRREL   *Glaucomys sabrinus*

Order: Rodentia (gnawing mammals). **Family:** Sciuridae (squirrels).
Range and habitat: south central and southeastern Alaska; in coniferous
forests. **Size and weight:** 10 inches; 3 ounces. **Diet:** bark, fungi, lichen,
insects, and birds' eggs. **Sounds:** generally silent; makes a "click" sound
when landing on a tree.

Many people in Alaska are unaware of the northern flying squirrel's
presence. These aerial creatures sleep all day and go about their activities
at night. A silky-gray, fur-covered membrane extends between the animal's
front and hind paws. Add to this its flattened tail, which acts like a rudder,
and you have a square-shaped creature well adapted for hang-gliding from
tree to tree or tree to ground.

If you happen to knock against or cut down one of the hollow trees in
which this species is fond of nesting, and if the squirrel that runs out is *small*
and a medium grayish brown, it's likely you've had a rare glimpse of a
flying squirrel.

During summer, flying squirrels don't leave much evidence of their
passage. They live mostly in trees, using the fur-covered membrane that
extends along each side of the body from the front to the rear legs to glide
between trees and occasionally from tree to earth, where they usually leave
no marks on the ground cover of their forest habitat. On snow, however,
their tracks can be identified because they lead away from what looks like
a miniature, scuffed snow-angel, the pattern left when a flying squirrel
lands at the end of an aerial descent. The tracks may wander around a bit
if the squirrel has foraged for morsels, but they will lead back to the trunk
of a nearby tree before long.

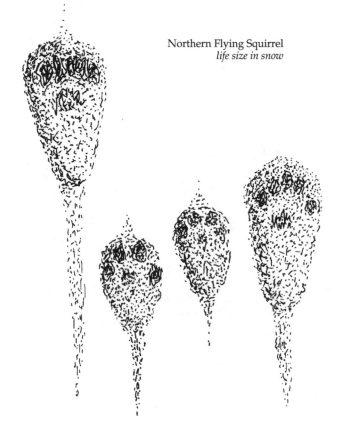

Northern Flying Squirrel
life size in snow

MINK

Mustela vison

Order: Carnivora (flesh-eating mammals). **Family:** Mustelidae (weasels and skunks). **Range and habitat:** absent only from the extreme northern coastal plain; in woodland areas near streams, lakes, and other bodies of water. **Size and weight:** 24 inches; 3 pounds. **Diet:** fish, frogs, salamanders, snakes, water birds, eggs, and all smaller mammals. **Sounds:** squeals, hisses.

The mink is the sleekest, most exuberant of the weasels, and the most aquatic. About the size of a small cat and medium brown all over, it is an excellent swimmer and may wander several miles a day searching for food along stream- and riverbanks and around the shorelines of lakes. Its den, too, is usually in a stream- or riverbank, an abandoned muskrat nest, or otherwise near water. Generally a nocturnal hunter, its tracks are likely to be the only indication you will have of its presence.

The mink leaves either groups of four tracks, such as those illustrated, or the characteristic double pair of tracks, usually not more than 26 inches apart. The tracks nearly always run along the edge of water. Though it has five toes both front and rear, it is quite common for only four-toed imprints to be apparent. Like all mustelids, the mink employs its scent glands to mark territory; so, as you track it through its hunting ranges, you may notice a strong scent here and there, different but as potent as that of its relative the skunk. You might also, in snow, find signs of prey being dragged, invariably leading to the animal's den.

Mink
life size in mud

37

MUSKRAT   *Ondatra zibethica*

Order: Rodentia (gnawing mammals). **Family:** Cricetidae (New World rats and mice). **Range and habitat:** absent only from the northern coastal plain; in fresh-water marshes, streams, lakes, and ponds. **Size and weight:** 24 inches; 3 pounds. **Diet:** omnivorous including aquatic plants and small aquatic animals such as snails, tadpoles, and shellfish, particularly fresh-water mussels. **Sounds:** high-pitched squeals.

The muskrat is a large rat modified for an aquatic life by the addition of a flattened, scaly, rudderlike tail and partially webbed hind feet. Like the beaver, it has been a commercially important fur bearer for several centuries. Muskrats associate readily with beavers and occasionally nest within the confines of beaver lodges. Most of the time they burrow into riverbanks or construct lodges similar to the beavers', but smaller and made of lighter materials, primarily grasses. They are basically nocturnal, but can be seen occasionally during the day or at dusk, parting the still surface of the water, tail sculling along, mouth full of grass for its nest.

Muskrat tracks are nearly always found in mud close to water. It is one of the few rodents with five toes on its front feet, although the small inner toe often fails to leave a mark. At the water's edge, the muskrat leaves tracks 2 to 3 inches apart when walking, 12 inches when running. The hind foot tracks are most distinctive, with the tail sometimes dragging. The hind feet have a stiff webbing of hair between the toes.

Muskrat
life size in mud

HOARY MARMOT
Mountain marmot

Marmota caligata

Order: Rodentia (gnawing mammals). **Family:** Sciuridae (squirrels). **Range and habitat:** widespread throughout southeastern, south, and central Alaska; in talus slopes and boulder fields, often in rocks and amid steep hillside forests and higher-altitude areas. **Size and weight:** 30 inches; 15 pounds. **Diet:** strictly herbivorous, including foliage and succulent alpine grasses and flowers. **Sounds:** a high, plaintive, drawn-out whistle.

The largest American squirrel, the hoary marmot sleeps more than any other mammal on the continent, hibernating from October through April, and sleeping at night during its short summer. It is covered with light gray fur and has black feet and black and white face markings. Fairly easy to find in the wild, it gives its location away with its piercing whistle, employed as both an alarm and as a means of keeping tabs on its fellow marmots' locations. A marmot's favorite daytime activities are eating and sunbathing on a prominent lookout rock. Its eyesight is not particularly good. If you stay downwind and move slowly, you should have no trouble sneaking in for a closer look.

The four front toes and five rear ones are typically rodent; the heel pads of the front feet are distinctive. The hoary marmot's tracks are identical to those of its cousin, the woodchuck (groundhog), who lives in some of the lowlands of east-central Alaska. The habitat will usually help you identify the track owner.

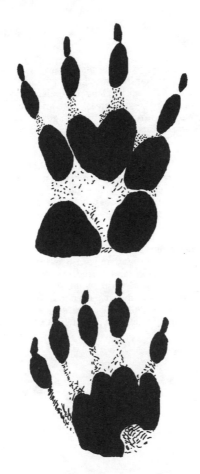

Hoary Marmot
life size in mud

41

MARTEN
Pine marten, sable   *Martes americana*

Order: Carnivora (flesh-eating mammals). **Family:** Mustelidae (weasels and skunks). **Range and habitat:** throughout most of Alaska except the southwestern and northern coastal plains; in coniferous forests and adjoining areas, occasionally rock-slide areas. **Size and weight:** 24 inches; 5 pounds. **Diet:** generally carnivorous, including mice, rats, squirrels, and small birds and eggs; berries and nuts. **Sounds:** generally silent.

Between a mink and fisher in size, the marten is typically weasel in appearance, with buff fur on its throat and light yellow-brown fur overall. It is an adaptable, energetic, solitary animal that is usually nocturnal and always extremely wary, and thus is sighted infrequently in the wild. Marten cover distances of many miles in a single night's hunting. They are active all year, denning in tree cavities or on the ground. They are great tree climbers and are largely arboreal, not the least oriented toward aquatic environs, although they are found in areas where dense coniferous forest extends right to the ocean's edge.

Marten leave few signs other than tracks, and these are scarce before snow falls. Then, their tracks tend to lead to and from trees and rarely venture near water, as the mink's usually do. Small, thin pads behind five toes and nails are normally visible in marten tracks, with size and spacing definitely larger than mink. Walking tracks are 6 to 9 inches apart; running, 2 feet separating groups of four prints; leaping, pairs of overlapping prints 4 feet apart.

Marten
life size in mud

RED FOX

Vulpes vulpes

Order: Carnivora (flesh-eating mammals). **Family:** Canidae (dogs). **Range and habitat:** throughout Alaska except the northern coastal plain; in woodlands, open fringes, and especially in mountainous areas near timberland. **Size and weight:** 40 to 42 inches; 12 to 15 pounds. **Diet:** omnivorous, including small mammals, birds, insects, eggs, fruit, nuts, grains, and other forage. **Sounds:** a variety of doglike noises.

The intelligence of the fox has been celebrated in literature since Aesop recorded his fables in 500 B.C. The fox often finds food easily by following the trail of an animal, such as a wolverine, that has made a food cache. An adult red fox does not sleep in a den in the winter. It curls its comely white-tipped tail around its nose to form a warm furry package. The fox may become covered by snow during a storm; perhaps some of the small, snowy hummocks Alaskans see in winter are actually sleeping foxes.

The sleek little red fox usually leaves a distinctive, nearly straight line of tracks, the front track slightly wider than the rear. Its feet are quite furry, adapted to its habitat; as a result the prints of pads and toes are often indistinct unless the surface is quite firm, in which case only a partial pad imprint might appear, with toe prints clearly separate. The claws always leave marks; in deep snow the tail may brush over and obscure some of the finer points of the tracks. Red fox tracks could be mistaken for those of a small domestic dog or arctic fox, except that the fox's heel pad has a unique curved bar and the heel pads of domestic dogs tend to be longer, extending forward between the outer toes. Also, a walking red fox leaves tracks from 12 to 18 inches apart, a somewhat longer stride than that of a similar-sized domestic dog, or the smaller arctic fox. The arctic fox, which is all white in winter and grayish to bluish brown in summer, is smaller than the red fox and found only in the far north and west of Alaska.

Red Fox
life size in sand

ARCTIC FOX

Alopex lagopus

Order: Carnivora (flesh-eating mammals). **Family:** Canidae (dogs). **Range and habitat:** western and northern Alaska; on tundra, at or near forest fringe. **Size and weight:** 30 inches; 7 pounds. **Diet:** omnivorous, including carrion, lemmings, voles, ground squirrels, birds, eggs, fish, berries and other forage. **Sounds:** variety of doglike noises.

The arctic fox is a fox adapted to the extremes of its habitat (where it only gets warm enough to snow during the summer), including a compact body, short legs, rounded ears, and heavily furred paws. Its summer coat is rarely dark blue-gray in non-snow areas of its habitat, more commonly brown to gray above and white below; in winter, it is distinctively all-white.

Arctic foxes are normally somewhat solitary, but they will congregate around natural or man-made food sources. They den in river banks or hillsides, with separate summer and winter den sites. In general, populations of arctic fox fluctuate with lemming populations as do the lynx populations with those of the snowshoe hare, peaking about every four years, although the arctic fox's diet is more varied, and it has evolved the habit of storing excess food in permafrost in the summer to tide it over lean times. In winter, arctic foxes are sometimes sighted following polar bears, scavenging leftovers.

Arctic fox tracks are the same size and shape as those of the red fox, but lack the bar on the heel pads. The densely haired foot pads often leave slightly blurred tracks even on ideal surfaces. Tracks like these north of the Brooks Range must have been left by an arctic fox. In the west, its range overlaps with that of the red fox. There, if you cannot find a very clear hind foot track, the spacing may be the only clue; the shorter-legged arctic fox leaves walking tracks from 8 to 12 inches apart.

Arctic Fox
life size in mud

COYOTE
Brush wolf, prairie wolf

Canis latrans

Order: Carnivora (flesh-eating mammals). **Family:** Canidae (dogs). **Range and habitat:** most of central, south, and southeastern Alaska; prefers open areas; extremely adaptable. **Size and weight:** 4 feet; 40 pounds. **Diet:** omnivorous, including fruit and berries, insects, fish, birds, mice, ground squirrels, other small mammals, and carrion. **Sounds:** barks, growls; packs yelp in high-pitched chorus.

Coyotes are important controllers of small rodents and are expanding their range. They are very smart, adaptable animals, good runners and swimmers, and have great stamina. Yet they are shy, and you will be lucky to see one in the wild.

Typically canine, the coyote's front paw is slightly larger than the rear, and the front toes tend to spread wider. The outer toes are often slightly larger than the inner toes on each foot. Toenails nearly always leave imprints, and the shape of coyote pads is unique, the front differing markedly from the rear. This characteristic, plus the lengthy stride (16 inches walking and leaps to 10 feet), may help you to distinguish their tracks from those of foxes or domestic dogs. Also, coyotes carry their tails down, leaving imprints in deep snow, and tend to walk in a straight line for longer distances than domestic dogs.

Coyote
life size in mud

49

PORCUPINE
Porky, quill pig

Erethizon dorsatum

Order: Rodentia (gnawing mammals). **Family:** Erethizontidae (porcupines). **Range and habitat:** common throughout most of Alaska except the far northern and western coasts; in forests, fields, semidesert; a very adaptable animal. **Size and weight:** 36 inches; 25 pounds average, some reach 40 pounds. **Diet:** strictly vegetarian, including succulents, willow leaves, bark, fruits, nuts, and many wild flowers. **Sounds:** generally quiet, but capable of a great variety of grunts, whines, and many harmonicalike noises; also clicks teeth together rapidly.

Porcupines are one of the few animals whose tracks you can follow with reasonable expectation of sighting their maker, because they move quite slowly when not alarmed, are often out during daylight hours, and do not see well. So if you stay downwind and are quiet, you can usually observe these peaceable animals at your leisure. An alarmed porcupine climbs a tree to escape danger and uses its quills only as a last-ditch defense against an outright attack.

Porcupines may be slow moving, but they are actually quite intelligent. I rescued an injured, week-old porcupine from the middle of a road once. It had problems with its feet and could not be expected to survive in the wilderness. So it lived in my house for two years, proving to be a wonderful pet. It had a wide range of emotions, loved to be handled, and never bored my guests.

Often the distinctive shuffling gait and dragging whisk-broom tail may be the only clear track signs, especially in deep snow. In winter the porcupine trail generally leads to and ends at a large coniferous tree. Once in a while a flat piece of snow or mud that has adhered to the porcupine's foot will be dislodged intact, revealing the unique pebbled texture of its sole. Imprints from the long claws may also be present.

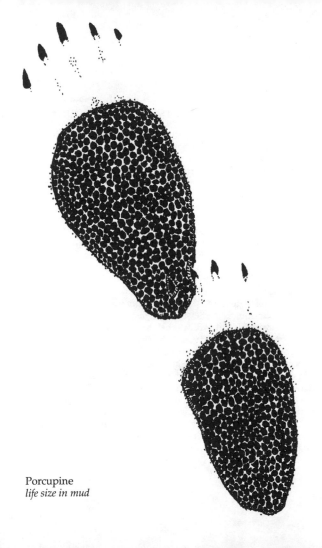

Porcupine
life size in mud

RIVER OTTER
Land otter

Lutra canadensis

Order: Carnivora (flesh-eating mammals). **Family:** Mustelidae (weasels and skunks). **Range and habitat:** widespread south of the Brooks Range; in or near lakes, streams, and coastal ocean areas. **Size and weight:** 4 feet; 20 pounds. **Diet:** fish, turtles, frogs, crayfish, snakes, birds and their eggs. **Sounds:** chirps, chatters, chuckles, and grunts.

On a sub-zero day in January, I had the pleasure of observing a river otter near the inlet of a frozen lake. Even out of water it retained its fluid gracefulness. Its neck arched in the lifting movements that are uniquely its own. There were black strips on the ice where the snow had been scraped away as the otter slid on its belly, revealing an innate sense of playful fun.

River otters will play both in and out of the water, alone or in the company of others. I once watched a group of otters curling around each other to form a large roly-poly ball of wriggling brown fur. On another occasion, I counted seven otters slithering and cavorting over one another in the ocean, looking like one multi-tailed, multi-headed sea monster.

An otter seen in salt water is not necessarily a sea otter. River otters are common in many coastal areas and they often enter the ocean in search of food. The style of swimming is the key to identification—a sea otter swims on its back, propelling itself with its flipperlike back feet; a river otter swims face down, with only its head and part of its back out of the water.

Sea otters are sea mammals in every sense—they eat, play, groom, and sleep in the ocean; they do go ashore at times, to escape violent storm conditions for example, but they never venture more than a few feet from the water, leaving few recognizable marks in their passage. The river otter is primarily a land animal. The webs of the rear feet may leave distinctive marks in soft mud, damp sand, or snow. The track imprints are roundish, with five front and hind toes usually showing clearly. River otters normally leave groups of four tracks, 13 to 30 inches apart, but can leap to 8 feet and slide for great distances on their undersides.

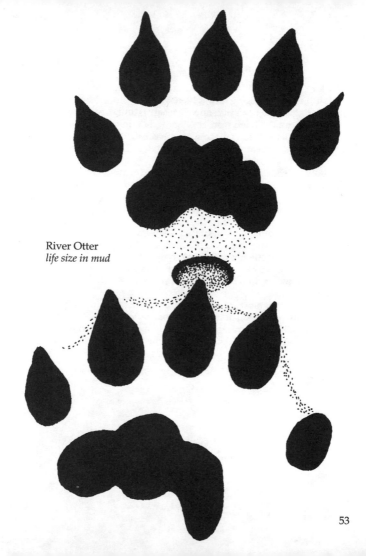

River Otter
life size in mud

53

LYNX

Felis lynx

Order: Carnivora (flesh-eating mammals). **Family:** Felidae (cats). **Range and habitat:** wide-ranging throughout Alaska; in forested woodlands and swamp fringes, wherever the snowshoe hare is found. **Size and weight:** 36 inches; 30 pounds. **Diet:** primarily snowshoe hares; occasionally other small mammals and birds. **Sounds:** quite vocal, including hisses, spitting noises, growls, caterwauls, and other generic cat-family noises.

Closely related to the bobcat in both size and characteristics, the lynx has adapted to its generally more northerly range with longer legs, longer and denser fur, and larger, thickly furred paws that provide buoyancy in deep snow and make it an excellent swimmer; conspicuous black ear tufts also distinguish it from the bobcat, whose range it does overlap. The lynx relies on the snowshoe hare as its dietary mainstay, and its range precisely overlaps the wilder, more remote portions of the hare's range. When the cyclical hare population is at its peak, lynxes have larger litters, but when the hares are scarce, the cats bear fewer offspring. The lynx hunts on the ground, but will go into trees to catch prey or to wait for ground animals to pass beneath.

The wary lynx is most active at night; by day, it tends to rest somewhere, venturing out only to kill unlucky prey that happen by, so you will seldom see it in the wild, but its tracks are unique. Lynx trails are about 7 or 8 inches wide, and its walking stride is around 12 inches.

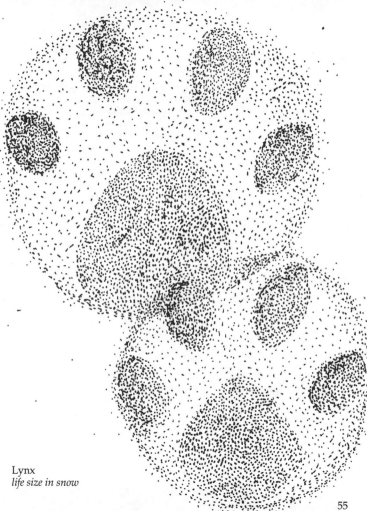

Lynx
life size in snow

MULE DEER
Blacktail deer, Sitka deer

Odocoileus hemionus

Order: Artiodactyla (even-toed hoofed animals). **Family:** Cervidae (deer). **Range and habitat:** common throughout the coast and offshore islands of southeastern Alaska; in forest and adjoining areas at all altitudes. **Size and weight:** 6 feet; 200 pounds. **Diet:** strictly vegetarian, including leaves, grasses, grains, and terminal shoots. **Sounds:** generally silent.

The mule deer in Alaska is somewhat smaller than the mule deer of the Rocky Mountain region, but it is now considered the same species. Active during the day and at dusk, it is fairly easy to spot in the wild and hard to confuse with any other animal. These deer are usually solitary or gather in small groups. At first sign of a threat they flee in their distinctive, feet-together, bounding gait, with all four hooves landing and taking off at the same time. They are strong swimmers and like salt, so they can often be seen along ocean beaches, especially during the winter.

The mule deer's tracks are easy to identify: the small, slender hooves usually spread slightly at the heels and the dewclaws usually leave imprints. They leave tracks fewer than 2 feet apart when walking or in clusters every 9 to 12 feet when bounding.

Mule Deer
life size in mud

MOUNTAIN GOAT

Oreamnos americanus

Order: Artiodactyla (even-toed hoofed animals). **Family:** Bovidae (cattle, sheep, and goats). **Range and habitat:** southeastern Alaska; in mountainous regions, steep, high pastures, and rocky areas, usually just below snowline; often descending to sea level in winter. **Size and weight:** 5 feet; 250 pounds. **Diet:** strictly vegetarian, including grass, leaves, sedges, and lichen. **Sounds:** generally silent.

Mountain goats are stocky, heavily muscled animals with white fur coats and short black horns. Their hooves are superbly adapted for the mountainous terrain in which they live. A combination of hard outer edge and soft inner part affords them the animal-equivalent of rock-climbing shoes, and the only thing that can catch a healthy mountain goat in rocky areas is another goat. But even mountain goats hit loose holds now and then, and the resulting falls can be fatal. Consequently, these animals prefer to spend their time grazing high alpine pastures with a sentry or two posted, the herd returning to the rocks to escape wolves, biting flies, or wildlife photographers, none of which really bother them to any great extent.

Mountain goat tracks are fairly common near high alpine ponds and patches of dirt around the rocky areas they inhabit. Winter snows often force them down into deer country, but their tracks are always easy to identify because of the splayed hooves, lack of dewclaw imprints, and mode of running.

Mountain Goat
life size in mud

WOLVERINE
Skunk bear   *Gulo gulo*

Order: Carnivora (flesh-eating mammals). **Family:** Mustelidae (weasels and skunks). **Range and habitat:** rare throughout Alaska; forest and adjoining areas, alpine meadows and tundra, near and above timberline. **Size and weight:** $3^1/_2$ feet; 40 pounds; largest of North American weasels. **Diet:** strictly carnivorous, including all smaller animals and carrion. **Sounds:** normally silent; may snarl or growl when disturbed.

The wolverine looks and acts like a small brown bear with a long, fluffy tail, buffy stripes down its sides, and a very nasty disposition. This fierce, aggressive animal is extremely strong for its size, and even the largest predators will avoid a confrontation with a healthy adult wolverine. A wary, secretive animal inhabiting fairly remote and desolate places, it is infrequently sighted in the wild.

Once, on a mid-winter airplane flight, I spotted a wolverine on a high Alaskan lake. As I circled and landed on the windswept ice, the alarmed wolverine arched its back and danced sideways much like a cat might, leaving all manner of irregular-looking tracks, before disappearing into some nearby boulders. The tracks were the size of a wolf's, but even where the fifth toe didn't leave a print, the pad shape was still unique. The wolverine walks flat-footed, and if not all of its soles leave marks, at least the heel knob behind the main pad usually does. At the same spot I noted an interesting phenomenon in some older tracks: the wolverine's weight had compressed the snow beneath its feet, then the wind had blown away the soft, untracked snow around the imprint, leaving perfect tracks standing an inch above the lake ice.

Native Alaskans consider it very unlucky to kill the magical wolverine. I've only known one person who killed one, a wolverine that could not be driven away from his food cache. An hour later, his airplane crashed while taking off. Ancient legends should always be respected.

Wolverine
1/2 life size in mud

GRAY WOLF   *Canis lupus*
Timber Wolf

Order: Carnivora (flesh-eating mammals). **Family:** Canidae (dogs).
Range and habitat: widespread throughout Alaska; in forested and open
areas from sea level to far above timberline. **Size and weight:** 6 feet; 150
pounds. **Diet:** generally carnivorous, including meat in any available form,
from mouse to moose; some insects, vegetation, fruits, and berries. **Sounds:**
barks, snarls, and growls; also long, mournful wail at night, not usually in
chorus like coyotes.

A person who sights a gray wolf in the wild these days is fortunate
indeed, for they have been systematically exterminated in most inhabited
areas of the continent.

Gray wolves are intelligent, gregarious animals that mate for life and
have relatively complicated social organizations. They seem to deserve
protection from eradication. I have been quite close to these wolves on
many occasions and can attest to the fact that they pose no threat to humans.
The encounters have always been exciting and pleasurable.

Wolf tracks show the four toes and nails typical of all canines, with the
front foot slightly larger than the rear. Angularity of pads and overall size
distinguish wolf tracks, as no other canine leaves tracks 5 or more inches in
length, nor covers ground like the gray wolf. Running wolves cover 6 to 8
feet every four steps, with a walking stride of nearly 2 feet.

Gray Wolf
1/2 life size in mud

DALL SHEEP
Mountain sheep

Ovis dalli

Order: Artiodactyla (even-toed hoofed mammals). **Family:** Bovidae (cattle, sheep, and goats). **Range and habitat:** central and southern Alaska; in mountainous, sparsely populated terrain, avoiding forested areas. **Height and weight:** 40 inches at shoulder; 150 pounds. **Diet:** variety of high-altitude browse, grasses, herbs, and lichen. **Sounds:** loudest and most recognizable are the sounds of head and horn butting made by competing rams during late fall; coughs, grunts, and bleating.

This big sheep, with its distinctive white coat and heavy coiled horns, lives in remote areas, where its hooves with their hard outer edges and spongy centers give it excellent agility on rocky surfaces. It tends to prefer high mountain meadows and scree slopes. In the summer, you'll commonly see groups of about ten ewes and lambs grazing or lying around chewing their cuds. In fall, rams join the herd, which may grow in size to 100 animals or more. The most distinctive behavior of the rams is the frenzied, high-speed head butting engaged in during the autumn mating season; noise from the impact carries a great distance in the open mountain country. Thanks to nature documentaries shown on television, people have had the opportunity to witness this head-butting ritual without having to venture into remote mountainous wildlands, thus saving wear and tear on fragile ecosystems and human knee joints.

Because of their range and habitat, Dall sheep leave tracks rarely confused with those of other hoofed animals. The hooves average 3½ inches in length, not as big as those of moose. Rather blunt and square, the hooves may show signs of wear and tear from the scree slopes; dewclaw prints are never left.

Dall Sheep
life size in mud

CARIBOU

Rangifer tarandus

Order: Artiodactyla (even-toed hoofed mammals). **Family:** Cervidae (deer). **Range and habitat:** widespread except in southwestern and southeastern Alaska; on tundra and taiga, extending into coniferous fringe areas. **Size and weight:** 3 to 4 feet at shoulder; 500+ pounds. **Diet:** succulent vegetation, lichens, fungi, willow twigs, and berries; also dropped caribou antlers. **Sounds:** generally quiet but capable of loud snorts.

The caribou of Alaska is the same species as the domesticated reindeer of Europe and Asia. A shaggy brown deerlike animal with a lighter neck and mane, white belly, rump, and tail, males and most females grow large antlers. The caribou is a good swimmer, gaining buoyancy from the air-filled hollow hairs of its coat. It can run at speeds of nearly 50 miles per hour for short distances. Bulls battle for harems of twelve to fifteen cows each fall. Its chief enemies are human hunters. Among the most migratory of all mammals, the caribou often form groups of up to 100,000 animals for spring and fall movements of hundreds of miles.

Both musk-ox and bison tracks might be mistaken for caribou. Those of the caribou are slimmer and nearly always exhibit dewclaw marks (see Musk-ox).

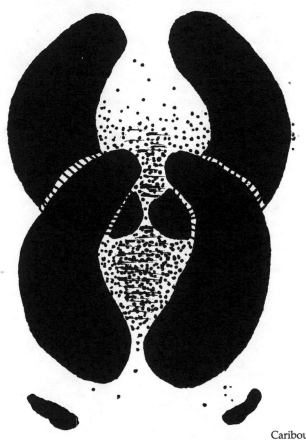

Caribou
½ life size in mud

MUSK-OX

Ovibos moschatus

Order: Artiodactyla (even-toed hoofed mammals). **Family:** Bovidae (bison, goats, sheep, cattle, and oxen). **Range and habitat:** along the Arctic coast; from arctic tundra and muskeg meadows to windswept hilltops and slopes where vegetation is exposed in winter. **Height and weight:** 3 to 5 feet at shoulder; 400 to 900 pounds. **Diet:** succulent vegetation, moss, lichen, and twigs. **Sounds:** occasional snorting or bellowing when excited.

The musk-ox is a very dark brown ox with shaggy hair hanging nearly to the ground, a real Ice-Age holdover of which there are only about 25,000 remaining in North America. Musk-oxen usually gather together into herds of up to 100 animals, and only range about 50 miles each year. They are best known for their soft, valuable underwool, called quiviut, which is woven by Eskimo people, and for their defensive circle with which they confront the occasional wolf or human, with calves on the inside and adults, heads lowered, in a formidable outer ring. The musk-ox has no musk glands; the strong odor from which it derives its name is caused by urine.

There are a few small herds of bison in central Alaska that leave nearly identical tracks to those of the musk-ox. The ranges do not overlap, however, so you will have no trouble determining which animal left tracks that look like these.

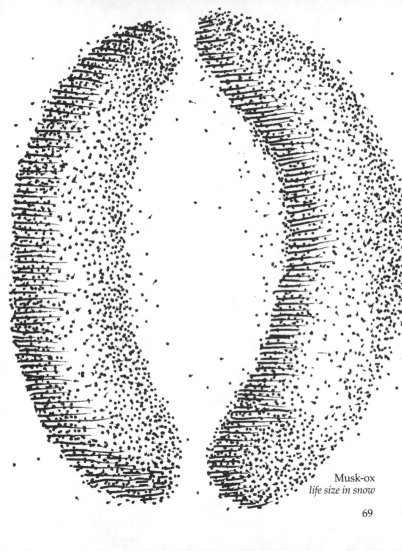

Musk-ox
life size in snow

BISON   *Bison bison*
Buffalo

Order: Artiodactyla (even-toed hoofed animals). **Family:** Bovidae (bison, goats, sheep, cattle, and oxen). **Range and habitat:** isolated herds at Copper River, Northway, and along the upper Kuskokwim from Farewell Lake to McGrath; on open grasslands and occasionally in woodlands and woodland fringes. **Height and weight:** 72 inches at shoulder; 2000 pounds. **Diet:** grazes mostly on grass; occasionally browses for buds, bark, twigs, shoots, and other vegetation. **Sounds:** a range of bovine noises.

Their dark brown, shaggy mane and beard, massive humped shoulders, and sharp, south, upturned horns make the great plains bison unmistakable. In 1880 more than 40 million bison grazed peacefully and stolidly in America, seldom taking notice of humans. Today there are 100,000 bison in the United States, largely captive and controlled in ten major public herds and many smaller private ones. They were reintroduced to Alaska in the 1930s.

Bison are quite gregarious animals—but it's a mistake to read meekness into the bison's seemingly mild-mannered indifference, however, because bison are huge and quick, quick enough to outrun a horse over a quarter-mile course. It's a good idea to treat a bison with the same respect and common sense you would any large domestic bull.

Because of specific herd locations in Alaska, chances are that you will know you are in bison territory and see the animals long before you find their tracks. Nevertheless, the tracks are a distinctive shape and size, measuring roughly 5 inches in each direction, with about 25 to 30 inches between walking track clusters. Bison also like to roll around, forming prominent dust wallows on the ground.

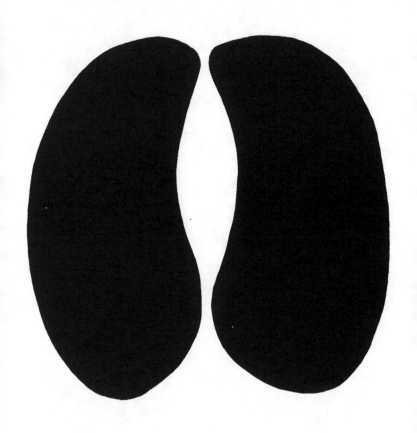

Bison
³/₄ life size in mud

71

MOOSE

Alces alces

Order: Artiodactyla (even-toed hoofed animals). **Family:** Cervidae (deer). **Range and habitat:** throughout most of Alaska except parts of the far western coast; in forests and adjoining areas, meadows, grasslands; often near rivers, lakes, and swampy bottomlands. **Height and weight:** 6 feet at shoulder; 800 to 1100 pounds. **Diet:** vegetarian, including aquatic plants, leafy succulents, twigs, bark, and terminal shoots. **Sounds:** generally silent, although both sexes capable of an astonishing range of whines, grunts, and other guttural sounds, especially during the fall mating season.

Their great size and peculiar shape distinguish the moose. Like all ruminant animals, they spend most of their waking hours slowly moving about and chewing. Their normal response to a perceived threat is to gallop wildly for a few hundred feet on legs marvelously adapted for running through high, thick brush, then to stop and resume their cud-chewing. Be that as it may, the bulls do put on quite a display in autumn, jousting with massive racks of antlers. But beware—they can be quite unpredictably aggressive toward humans at that time of year, as can a cow with a young calf in the spring.

Differentiating hoofed-animal tracks can be tricky, but there is no problem with adult moose tracks. They are strikingly large, from 5 to 7 inches in length and up to 4 feet apart even when walking. Juvenile tracks, however, can be confused with those of mule deer where their ranges overlap. But remember that juvenile animals almost always travel with an adult, so you must search the immediate area for larger tracks. Habitat will be a clue, also. No other Alaskan hoofed animal shares the moose's great affinity for water.

Finally, moose are not herd animals. A bull, cow, and two calves is as large as a moose gathering gets, whereas other Alaskan hoofed animals often congregate in larger numbers. Then again, four moose can make a lot of tracks by hanging around one small pond for an extended period of time. But the size of the adult track should provide positive identification.

Moose
½ life size in mud

73

SNOWSHOE HARE

Lepus americanus

Order: Lagomorpha (rabbitlike mammals). **Family:** Leporidae (hares and rabbits). **Range and habitat:** throughout most of Alaska, except for major islands and parts of the western coast; forests, brushy areas, and swamps. **Size and weight:** 18 inches; 4 pounds. **Diet:** grasses, willows, lupine, and other vegetation; buds of conifers, twigs, bark of alders, aspens, and willows. **Sounds:** thumps its feet; also screams, grunts, and growls occasionally.

Most of you are probably familiar with the snowshoe hare—this medium-sized member of the rabbit family is active day and night, year-round, and is quite common over a large territory. It is aptly named since its unique hind feet have separable toes, allowing them to function like snowshoes when traveling on soft surfaces. In snowy areas the winter coat is white, changing predominantly to brown during the other seasons.

Although its range partially overlaps that of the northern hare, track recognition is easy, because of the natural snowshoe formed by its toes. A snowshoe hare's toes always spread out, leaving distinctively separate imprints. The length of each track pattern of four prints averages 11 inches; hopping length is about 14 inches, while leaping distance is more than 5 feet.

The northern hare is a lot longer than its Alaskan cousin, and lives along the western coastal area of the state, in open tundra. Its tracks are smaller and narrower individually, while the width of the straddle, length of pattern, and leaping distances are all usually greater.

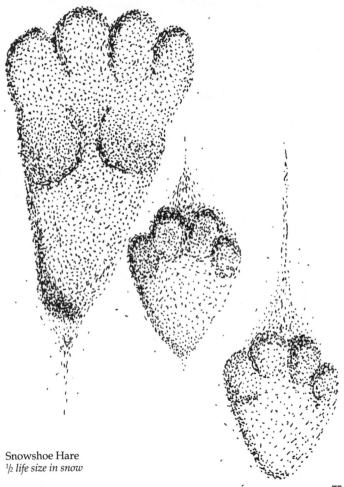

Snowshoe Hare
½ life size in snow

BEAVER

Castor canadensis

Order: Rodentia (gnawing mammals). **Family:** Castoridae (beavers). **Range and habitat:** widespread throughout all central, southern, and southeastern Alaska; in marshes, streams, and lakes with brush and trees, or in open forest along riverbanks. **Size and weight:** 36 inches; 55 pounds. **Diet:** aquatic plants, bark, and the twigs and leaves of many shrubs and trees, preferably alder, cottonwood, and willow. **Sounds:** nonvocal, but smacks tail on water surface quite loudly to signal danger.

This industrious, aquatic mammal is the largest North American rodent. Although it sometimes lives unobtrusively in a riverbank, usually it constructs the familiar beaver lodge, a roughly conical pile of brush, stones, and mud extending as much as 6 feet above the surface of a pond, and gnaws down dozens of small softwood trees with which it builds a conspicuous system of dams, often several hundred yards long. A beaver can grasp objects with its front paws and stand and walk upright on its hind feet. It uses its flat, scaly, strong tail for support out of water and as a rudder when swimming. Gregarious animals, beavers work well together on their collective projects. They are active day and night year-round, but may operate unobserved beneath the ice during much of the winter, using subsurface lodge entrances.

If you are lucky, the large, webbed hind foot tracks left by a beaver will be clear, with 6 to 8 inches between pairs. Beavers frequently, however, obscure part or most of their tracks by dragging their tails and / or branches over them. Still, the large webbed hind feet almost always leave distinctive whole or partial imprints.

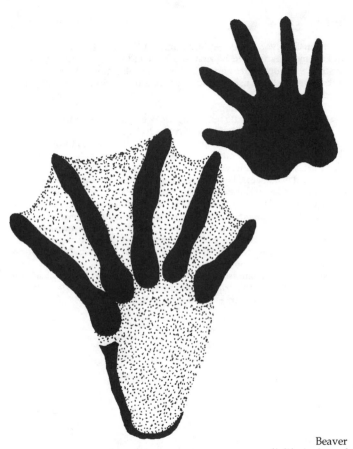

Beaver
1/2 life size in mud

SEA OTTER   *Enhydra lutris*

Order: Carnivora (flesh-eating mammals). **Family:** Mustelidae (weasels and skunks). **Range and habitat:** southern and southeastern coastal waters; salt water only. **Size and weight:** 40 inches; 40 pounds. **Diet:** mollusks, crabs, other shellfish, fish, and other marine animals. **Sounds:** hisses loudly when alarmed.

The sea otter is an agile and energetic ocean-living otter that has lived along the west coast of America since the Ice Age. Its real troubles began when its fur became the royal fur of China; in the first half of the nineteenth century, Russian and Aleut fur hunters nearly exterminated the animals. Since 1911, sea otters have been protected by a variety of international treaties and U.S. federal laws, were transplanted back into Alaskan waters at various places, and their numbers and range are now expanding.

Sea otters are born buoyant as corks, learn to swim quickly, and spend their lives inconspicuously among offshore rocks or patches of floating vegetation. They are among the few species of tool-using mammals worldwide; you might occasionally hear or observe a sea otter floating on its back and breaking a shellfish open with a stone brought up from the bottom expressly for that purpose.

Sea otters don't come ashore very often, but when they do, they leave the only readily identifiable tracks of all the sea mammals that visit Alaska's shores, primarily six species of true and eared seals.

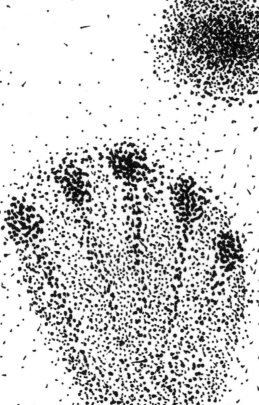

Sea Otter
1/2 life size in sand

BLACK BEAR
Cinnamon bear, glacier bear

Ursus americanus

Order: Carnivora (flesh-eating mammals). **Family:** Ursidae (bears). **Range and habitat:** widespread throughout central, southern, and southeastern Alaska; in forests and adjoining areas at all elevations. **Size and weight:** 7 feet; 450 pounds. **Diet:** omnivorous, including fish, small mammals, insects, fruit, berries, and succulent vegetation. **Sounds:** usually silent; grunts, whines, growls, clicks teeth, smacks jaw—all danger signals for smaller animals, including humans.

The black bear is the smallest and most common Alaskan bear. Smokey is a black bear, and we have grown accustomed to seeing these animals around rural garbage dumps and parks. In the wild, black bears are shy and wary of human contact and, consequently, harder to sight. They are good tree climbers, swim well, and can run 25 miles per hour for short stretches. They are very quick and strong. It could be dangerous to underestimate any black bear, and downright unhealthy to get too close to a mother bear with cubs.

Black bear tracks are usually impossible to mistake, being nearly human in both size and shape. The large claws leave prints wherever the toes do. Occasionally I have seen places where a bear has slipped on firm mud; its toes and claws did not register, but the smooth slide mark from the sole of the foot was distinctive. Be alert for small tracks, just the size of my drawing—you really don't want to get tangled up with those cubs!

Black Bear
¹/₂ life size in mud

BROWN BEAR
Grizzly bear

Ursus arctos

Order: Carnivora (flesh-eating mammals). **Family:** Urisdae (bears). **Range and habitat:** widespread throughout Alaska including many off-shore islands; alpine meadows, prairies, and forested areas from sea level to above timberline. **Size and weight:** 8 to 11 feet; 800 to 1600 pounds. **Diet:** omnivorous, including nearly any edible material, fish, small and some large mammals, birds, insects, fruits, berries, nuts, and succulent vegetation. **Sounds:** mostly silent, but may grunt, growl, chop jaws, and click teeth together when annoyed or alarmed.

If you are looking down at tracks over a foot long that look remotely like the ones illustrated, you've gotten yourself into brown bear country. Most people are beginning to agree that the hundred-odd variations on the "large brown hairy creature" theme are all the same animal. The brown bears of the Alaskan coast tend to be larger and more reclusive, while those of the inland areas, commonly called grizzlies, are slightly smaller and generally more aggressive. But all brown bears have certain things in common: they are large beasts with prominent shoulder humps; they are very territorial; their behavior is unpredictable under the best circumstances; their eyesight is poor; they are faster and stronger than you'd expect; and they've killed and eaten animals larger than you.

In brown bear country, sane people walk slowly, talk and whistle, shake cans full of pebbles, and tie bells on their packs. Prolonged observations are best conducted from trees, as brown bears don't climb.

Tracks like these found along the Arctic coast during mid-summer may have been made by a polar bear, the great white bear we all know from zoos and movies, who sometimes comes ashore from the pack ice. The polar bear is the most carnivorous Alaskan bear and can be very aggressive and dangerous, but it is so rare ashore as to pose very little danger to most humans.

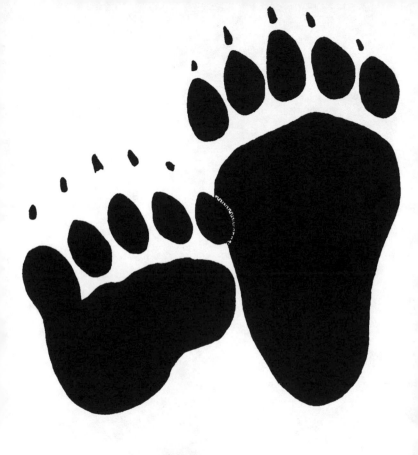

Brown Bear
$^1/_4$ *life size in mud*

83

Birds

NORTHERN JUNCO

Junco hyemalis

Order: Passeriformes (perching birds). **Family:** Fringillidae (buntings, finches, and sparrows). **Range and habitat:** summers throughout the state, winters in the southeast; common in and near coniferous forests, weedy fields, and brushy forest fringes. **Size and weight:** length 6 inches, wing-span 8 inches; less than 1 ounce. **Diet:** seeds, insects, and berries. **Sounds:** chips and trills.

The junco is a common and wide-ranging little bird. Small flocks of gray, brown, and white juncos moving about in search of seeds on the surface of winter snow are a common sight throughout most of southeastern Alaska, as is the network of interlaced tracks these and other small birds leave beneath bird feeders. Juncos are attracted to the seeds that chickadees scatter while looking for sunflower seeds in the standard wild bird mix; they may be accompanied by an occasional sparrow during their winter outings.

Junco tracks are typical of the vast number of smaller land birds that leave delicate lines on snow, sand, or mud of inland areas. Hind toes are about twice as long as front toes, and the tracks are found in pairs spaced up to 5 inches apart, as these birds hop instead of walk. The relative size of the tracks will give a clue to the identity of the maker, as will habitat and seasonal considerations, verified, of course, by actual field sightings.

Relatively few small land birds remain in Alaska year-round, however. Tracks like these in snow elsewhere in the state may have been left by chickadees, sparrows, snow buntings, crossbills, grosbeaks, or the common redpoll.

Northern Junco
life size in snow

COMMON FLICKER   *Colaptes auratus*

Order: Piciformes (woodpeckers and allies). **Family:** Picidae. **Range and habitat:** year-round resident of south central and southeastern Alaska; also found in the interior during summer months; in open country near and among large trees. **Size and weight:** length, 10 inches; wingspan, 14 inches; 4 ounces. **Diet:** insects. **Sounds:** loud repeated flick or flicker; also shrill descending "kee-oo."

One of relatively few birds residing year-round in Alaska, the flicker is most easily recognized by the black polka-dots on its white chest and belly, and the yellow or orange plumage under its wings. These jay-sized woodpeckers often fly down to the ground to eat ants and other insects and grubs.

Several other woodpeckers visit or reside in Alaska for parts of the year; all have feet of the same distinctive shape, adapted for clinging to tree trunks and limbs while the birds dig for wood-boring insects. But they rarely leave the trees, so when you find tracks like those illustrated, you can feel reasonably sure they were left by a ground-visiting flicker.

Common Flicker
life size in mud

WILLOW PTARMIGAN   *Lagopus lagopus*

Order: Galliformes (terrestrial birds). **Family:** Tetraonidae (turkeys, grouse, quail). **Range and habitat:** year-round resident throughout most of Alaska; in grasslands, tundra meadows, brush thickets, sheltered gullies, occasionally in pine forests during winter months. **Size and weight:** length 10 inches, wingspan 18 inches; 1 pound. **Diet:** twigs, leaves, buds, berries, and insects. **Sounds:** various distinctive machinelike growling cackles.

This grouselike bird is the state bird of Alaska. It wears a white plumage with black outer tail feathers during winter months, and molts to mottled brown with white wings and belly in summer. Ptarmigans are adroit at hiding among meadow foliage; you won't usually see them until they burst up and, flapping madly or soaring close to the ground, often making very peculiar noises, disappear over the next hummock. They never fly far, and you can spend as much of the day chasing them around as you want to. During the summer months it's not uncommon to find a hen with up to ten chicks dashing among tundra berries and low brush.

Willow ptarmigan tracks are uncommon during warm weather because of the nature of their habitat, but during winter months they are easy to locate, often accompanied by wing marks left at takeoff. Tracks like these might also have been made by the very similar Rock Ptarmigan, or by ruffed, sharp-tailed, or spruce grouse, all of which live year-round in portions of the state.

Willow Ptarmigan
life size in snow

COMMON SNIPE   *Capella gallinago*

Order: Charadriiformes (sandpipers, gullies, and allies). **Family:** Scolopacidae (snipes and sandpipers). **Range and habitat:** summers throughout most of Alaska; common in marshes and bogs and along riverbanks. **Size and weight:** length 12 inches, wingspan 16 inches; 4 ounces. **Diet:** insects, aquatic larvae, snails, earthworms, small crustacea, and seeds of marsh plants. **Sounds:** "shak" and "kzrrt"; winnowing during summer display flight.

The common snipe is recognized by its brown, streaked head and back, and in flight by its brown rump and orange tail. It flies in a rapid zigzag and generally stays close to cover. During spring and summer at dusk or on overcast days, the snipe makes a tremolo sound with its feathers as it flies; on moonlit nights this winnowing sound is wonderfully eerie, like the faraway laughter of a lunatic.

The snipe tracks illustrated here are typical of most shorebird tracks, which are usually found scattered in damp sand or across mudflats near salt water. The front center toe is longer than the two outer toes, and the small hind toe, more of a heel spur than a toe, leaves a small imprint. The tracks are usually printed in a line, only an inch or so apart for birds the size of the snipe, less for sandpipers, and up to 6 inches for birds the size of a greater yellowlegs.

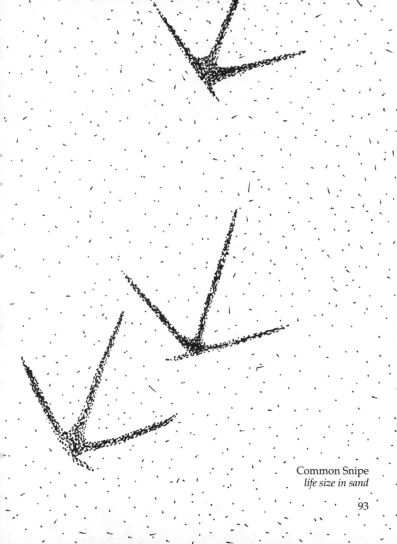

Common Snipe
life size in sand

COMMON RAVEN   *Corvus corax*

Order: Passeriformes. **Family:** Corvidae (jays, magpies, crows). **Range and habitat:** year-round resident through most of Alaska; very adaptable, usually in coniferous forests, along rocky coasts, and in other fairly wild areas. **Size and weight:** length 16 inches, wingspan to 30 inches; 1 pound. **Diet:** primarily a scavenger; also takes rodents, bird eggs and young, and large insects. **Sounds:** variety of hoarse croaking noises.

You'll often find ravens congregating to scold a porcupine, owl, or eagle in a tree, or soaring in flocks above a predator or some other interesting activity on the ground. This large black bird with the wedge-shaped tail and stout bill is impossible to confuse with any other Alaskan bird. It is generally wary of humans, however, and is most frequently sighted riding high air currents or performing a variety of aerial acrobatics and mock fighting with friends.

Raven tracks are usually clustered around a red stain on snow, or a shred of meat or bone on the ground, where these carnivorous birds have been picking some food prize apart. Tracks identical to these but smaller were probably made by gray jays or black-billed magpies, both of which are also common year-round residents throughout Alaska.

Common Raven
life size in mud

GREAT HORNED OWL
Cat owl

Bubo virginianus

Order: Strigiformes. **Family:** Strigidae (owls). **Range and habitat:** widespread throughout most of Alaska year-round; all habitats from forests to deserts with cliffs for nest sites. **Size and weight:** length 23 inches, wingspan 52 inches; $3^1/_2$ pounds. **Diet:** rabbits, mice, rats, voles, skunks, and grouse. **Sounds:** normally the male hoots four to five times while the female hoots six to eight times.

One spring day I spotted what looked like a cat sitting on a platform of sticks high up in a hemlock tree. It stared down at me with intense yellow eyes. This was a nesting "cat owl," more commonly called the great horned owl. The owl held the tufts of feathers on either side of its head in different positions, which made it look remarkably like a cat. These owls nest so early in the spring that the brooding female is often partially covered with snow. They prefer to use nests constructed in previous years by hawks or ravens, rather than building their own.

When owls leave their nests, they fly through the forest without a sound. Special modifications of their wing feathers allow these night hunters to travel the airways in silence.

Owl tracks are uncommon, but owls do come down to the ground and pause long enough to leave a few tracks occasionally. They land to investigate and feed on food items that are too heavy to carry away or don't inspire them to do so. Car-killed animals are a good example, and on recently rained-upon dirt roads, you may find owl tracks.

The tracks of the great horned owl in mud show the three thick and powerful talons it uses for grasping. The hind toe mark is just a small point.

Several other small owls reside in Alaska either year-round or during the summer, including short-eared, boreal, snowy, great gray, and hawk owls.

Great Horned Owl
life size in mud

CANADA GOOSE

Branta canadensis

Order: Anseriformes. **Family:** Anatidae (ducks, geese, and swans). **Range and habitat:** year-round resident of southeastern Alaska; on coastal mudflats, marshes, and lakes. **Size and weight:** length 3 feet, wingspan 5 feet; 14 pounds. **Diet:** eel grass, grain, seeds, plant shoots; also roots, tubers, and leaves from aquatic plants. **Sounds:** "uh-whonk, uh-whonk"; hisses when angry or alarmed.

Canada geese are commonly observed feeding in wet fields during early mornings and late afternoons, their black necks arching downwards to make strikingly curved patterns against the beige grass. When disturbed, they begin to call in unison, creating a wild cacophony of sound. Soon they take to the air, flying in V-shaped wedges.

Canadas mate for life. They nest on the ground near water, often choosing the small islets of beaver or muskrat houses as sites for their nests.

Typical of this family of birds, the Canada goose has four toes but the hind toe is elevated and does not leave an imprint. Its three main toes fan out in front and are connected by webs. The tracks are often seen on mud flats in conjunction with their squiggly sausage-shaped droppings.

During summer months, tracks of this style but relatively smaller may have been left by a great variety of ducks, murres, mergansers, cormorants, gulls, and terns that visit Alaska. Very few of these remain after the breeding season.

Canada Goose
life size in mud

GREAT BLUE HERON   *Ardea herodias*

Order: Ciconiiformes (herons and allies). **Family:** Ardeidae (herons, egrets, and bitterns). **Range and habitat:** year-round resident of southeastern Alaska; in fresh- and salt-water marshes, coastal mudflats, sand bars, shallow bays. **Size and weight:** length 4 feet, wingspan 6 feet; 7 pounds. **Diet:** fish, snakes, insects, mice, and frogs. **Sounds:** "kraak," strident honks.

The presence of a great glue heron magically transforms a landscape, adding an aura of quiet beauty comparable to that of a Japanese brush painting. The heron can be observed gracefully wading in shallow water as it seeks the fish that comprise a large part of its diet. A heron's nest, maintained year after year, is an elaborate structure of sticks 3 feet in diameter.

Great blue heron tracks are apt to be seen bordering the fresh- or salt-water areas where it feeds. It has four toes all on the same level. The hind toe is well developed for standing and walking. A claw imprint shows clearly at the end of each toe.

The sandhill crane is the only other wading bird in Alaska that leaves tracks of this size and style. These birds pass through southern portions of Alaska every year, on their way to nesting areas in the remote arctic tundra and muskeg plains of northern and eastern Alaska.

Great Blue Heron
life size in mud

101

GOLDEN EAGLE   *Aquila chrysaetos*

Order: Falconiformes (raptors). **Family:** Accipitridae (hawks, kites, and eagles). **Range and habitat:** year-round resident of most of Alaska, except north of the Brooks Range and southeastern Alaska; in remote mountains, grasslands, and forested areas. **Size and weight:** length 32 inches, wingspan more than 72 inches; 10 pounds. **Diet:** primarily rodents; occasionally other small mammals, birds, and fish. **Sounds:** rapid, sharp chips.

Both the adult and the immature golden eagle have a rich, dark brown body plumage; the golden neck feathers are visible only at close range. The broad white tail band and white wing patches of the immature bird are good field marks. These birds exhibit typical buteo flight, with very long rounded wings.

The golden eagle is rare and endangered; if you sight one or find its tracks, consider it a lucky day. The golden eagle's track shape—four equally prominent toe and claw imprints—is also representative of many species of hawks and falcons that are found within Alaska. The size and location of the tracks will vary depending on the particular species.

The bald eagle leaves identical tracks, and is very common year-round throughout southeastern Alaska. During the summer months, bald eagles are found in most of central and southern Alaska as well, and are likely to be more common than golden eagles during those months of nesting.

Golden Eagle
life size in mud

Recommended Reading

CARE OF THE WILD FEATHERED AND FURRED: A Guide to Wildlife Handling and Care, Mae Hickman and Maxine Guy (Unity Press, 1973); unique perspectives on animal behavior and emergency care of injured and orphaned wildlife.

A FIELD GUIDE TO ANIMAL TRACKS, Olaus J. Murie (Houghton Mifflin Co., Boston, 2nd ed., 1975); a classic work on track identification by Murie (1889-1963), an eminent naturalist and wildlife artist; one of the Peterson Field Guide Series; an excellent research text for home study.

ISLAND SOJOURN, Elizabeth Arthur (Harper & Row, 1980); an account of life on an island in British Columbia's wilderness, with a chapter devoted to a metaphysical perspective of animal tracks.

SNOW TRACKS, Jean George (E. P. Dutton, 1958); an introduction to the study of animal tracks for very young children.

THE TRACKER, Tom Brown and William J. Watkins (Berkley Publications, 1984); an intriguing story by a man who has devoted his life to the science of following tracks and other movement clues of various animals, including humans.

Index

About the author:

Chris Stall first became interested in wild country and wild animals during several years with a very active Boy Scout troop in rural New York State. Since then he has traveled and lived around most of North America, including eleven years in Alaska, studying, photographing, sketching, and writing about wild animals in their natural habitats. His photos and articles have appeared in a number of outdoor and nature magazines. Chris participated in a 1365-mile solo kayak journey down the Mississippi River to New Orleans in 1988 and a year of sailing around Central America in 1989–90.

Other books you may enjoy from The Mountaineers:

Alaska's Brooks Range: The Ultimate Mountains, Kauffmann. In-depth profile of one of the world's last, great, unspoiled wildernesses. Looks at geography, geology, exploration and human history, past and present conservation efforts.

Alaska's Parklands: The Complete Guide, Simmerman.
Revised edition covers every national and state park and wild area—locations, terrain, scenery, wildlife, outdoor activities available, camping, weather, facilities, access. Includes 34" x 48" full-color topographic map.

55 Ways to the Wilderness in Southcentral Alaska, 4th Edition, Nienhueser & Wolfe.
A year-round guide for hiking, skiing, and snowshoeing trips outside of Anchorage, to Kenai and Valdez.

Discover Southeast Alaska With Pack and Paddle, 2nd Edition, Piggott.
Contains details for 58 hikes in the area from Ketchikan to Skagway, plus a 12-day paddle trip from Juneau to Angoon.

Mt. McKinley: The Pioneer Climbs, Moore.
Features the highlights of climbs on McKinley from initial explorations up to the 1940's. Includes maps and historic photos.

John Muir: The Eight Wilderness-Discovery Books
First time in one volume: *The Story of My Boyhood and Youth; A Thousand Mile Walk to the Gulf; My First Summer in the Sierra; The Mountains of California; Our National Parks; The Yosemite; Travels in Alaska; Steep Trails.*

Other books in the *Animal Tracks* series:

Animal Tracks of Northern California
Animal Tracks of Southern California
Animal Tracks of the Great Lakes States
Animal Tracks of the Mid-Atlantic States
Animal Tracks of New England
Animal Tracks of the Pacific Northwest
Animal Tracks of the Rocky Mountains
Animal Tracks of the Southeast States
Animal Tracks of the Southwest
Animal Tracks of Texas

Two-color, 25" x 38" *Animal Tracks* posters are available for all the above except for Alaska, the Southwest, and Texas.

Available from your local bookstore or outdoor store, or from The Mountaineers Books, 1001 SW Klickitat Way, Suite 201, Seattle, WA 98134. Or call for a catalog of over 300 outdoor books: 1-800-553-4453.

Notes